C000010845

GRAVITY FOR BEGINNERS

Poetry by the same author

Kevin Crossley-Holland
Gravity for Beginners

NEW POEMS

2021

Published by Arc Publications,
Nanholme Mill, Shaw Wood Road
Todmorden OL14 6DA, UK
www.arcpublications.co.uk

978 1910345 39 9 (pbk)
978 1910345 82 5 (ebk)

Design by Tony Ward
Printed in Great Britain by TJ Books Limited, Padstow, Cornwall

Cover photograph:
'Mommet' by Andrew Rafferty,
reproduced by kind permission of the photographer

Supported using public funding by
ARTS COUNCIL
ENGLAND
LOTTERY FUNDED

**Arc Publications UK and Ireland Series:
Series Editor: Tony Ward**

for Stephen Stuart-Smith

with gratitude for making thy friends' books,
and thy books friends

CONTENTS

Das is der Sinn von allem, was einst war,
daß es nich bleibt mit seiner ganzen Schwere,
daß es zu unserm Wesen wiederkehre,
in uns verwoben, tief und wunderbar...

Vergangenheiten sind dir eingepflanzt,
um sich aus dir, wie Gärten, zu erheben.

*

This is the heart of everything that ever was
  – it does not last with all its mass
but returns to each of us, our very being,
  woven into us, profound and magical...

Times past have been planted within you
so that out of you, like a garden, they'll grow.

SEAHENGE: A JOURNEY

1. TUMP

Back again! Back
and up to that oval tump above the chalk cross
to search for a thumbnail of pottery,
a single sherd.
When I launched myself into the trench beside it,
packed with crackling beech-leaves,
I believed I was an inmate of the barrow.

Commentator, diplomat, viola player, priest
– all four beached on my limitations
and quickening sense of myself.
But why did I not train to be an archaeologist?

That riddled oak lectern,
and the scarabs and beads from Ur,
a nacreous perfume bottle lifted
from some settlement south of Alexandria…
Asking, deducing, dovetailing
past and present, matter and spirit:

my heart quickens
to Whiteleaf and my childhood museum,
that shed growing into the ground,

and with one eye on the threatening sky,
one on a molehill,
I brighten at the little finds
I'm still adding to it.

2. DEADHEADED

Undone, a necklace of rose lights
looping over the Chilterns
above the spring line
(no culture chooses to look down at its dead)
then on through the wilderness of this world
– the airy Downs, silly Suffolk –
each blossom radiant, fading,
deadheaded.

Sky widens, and the chain tautens.
Footfalls in the sandy soil and soggy fen,
footfalls through forests bedded
with cones and needles:
knappers and salt-panners and oyster-men,
truth-tellers, outcasts, devotees
still resting here.

Sudden gusts and bluster,
bolts of thunder, stinging rain,
and no less sudden,
wings of Chalk Hill blues again.

High over the henge and all its voices
there's a spray of lights, a cluster:
shoulder-companions on this last ridge
at the end of their long journey
– dark roses before the drop
to the baffled sea.

3. UNLIVING

With mommets and hodmedods
we tried to scare him away.
For a while we did.
Death flew off with his demons
and you burned brightly.

When we propped you
against the door-post
you heard your willow-daughter
comforting her daughter
who will soon be born.

You kept begging us
to call on our ancestors.
Flame-cheeks, twitch-fingers.
You kept saying the unliving
can guard the living.

4. Shimmer

All day you waited
outside your hut,
not alone,

and murmured and warbled
last words
before you lost your breath.

You watched how the ridge
grew holy
and how the end of the evening
shimmered
the bristling fields
copper and bronze

even your own messengers
the waves of the sky
no longer mud-foul
but oyster and pearl

while sea-eagles and harriers
before their bloody work
made low passes

5. Tree

When you came I was unborn.

No one knew your name
or where you had walked from.
'Along the living streams,' you said.

You told us there's a tree
opening over all that is
        all that is
– white skull, green earth, swarming sea.
'It sings and suffers for us.
It is our always tree.'

You said when our leader dies,
each of us is turned over, each broken.
You told us to smash all the death-urns
and nick the axe-blades
to set their spirits free,
then lay him in the cradle
of an upturned tree.

'Do this,' you said,
'and he will be sky-born again.
After the fire and flood
you too will be sky-born again.'

Our grandfathers and great grandmothers
laughed they cried
and in the rush-light
they asked you many questions.

I know I would have seen you
before sunrise
up there on the lopeway
just below the ridge.

6. ALTAR

I closed your lids
with this right thumb.
Then we fashioned your death-cradle.
The elders and the lame
with chains of song unbroken,
and the young splashing, delving, squeezing out,
then heaping up your island,
all the men and women with their singing axes.

With honeysuckle ropes we snared the posts
and set them up in trenches side by side.
Past the hazels and alders
we hauled the huge oak-stump
with its horn roots to the bog.
We chipped all the bark
from your cradle.
                    Your white altar.
                    Your shining altar.

From where sun dies the wind blew,
tides gulped and shunted
behind our dunes for many days.
But at last we lifted you
on thick green trusses and silver wormwood
we carried you out from the dead-house.
                    You wore flowers.
                    You wore flowers.

Sun-cups, silken cottongrass,
threaded and twisted,
starlight, marsh-mallow.
Your choker wreathen sea-pink.

So gently we laid you
on the crush of chalk and clay
between the roots
of the upturned tree.
                    Our death-baby.
                    Our death-baby.

Each of us sipped three sips
of the sweet water, the sweet water
lapping you.
And I, blood of your blood,
placed your death-gifts around you.

The sea-eagles and harriers heard our cries.
They cried with us.

Then each of us sang.
I sang I felt the darkness knotting
inside you.
I sang you were the setting sun.
I sang until I closed the lids
over your eyes
with this right thumb
sky always always shone in them.

7. CROSSING

Marram whipped, peat-lipped,
salt-scoured, windswept:
the earth meets the sea

and each opens to the running sky
and reflects it. Gazing across
the wash of years

we say this stark foreshore
where flux is the only constant
looks entirely fitting

as the site of a crossing-place;
and while we recognise
it's not what its makers intended

with their plans for circles and walkways
well-guarded by dunes,
and their heroic labour,

see also that time and dream
have mapped and remapped it
into another truth.

8. TIDES

Of what once was
what's left will soon be gone.

Without kicking up more waves
of argument and speculation,

or putting unanswerable
philosophical questions...

Still not knowing how not to look,
and not to ask but breathe

and have my own tides reveal
what they will and when they will.

Wrynecks drum, grey plovers whistle,
and boring piddocks have their way.

Of what once was
what's left will soon be gone.

Wholly to immerse myself
wholly to find myself.

Not to search for words words
but in this place only to be.

9. Burden

Not sorry and not stricken
but of age
I'll strip my scape
to headland
                    and heartland.

Let each silence
                    and breath
each word-in-waiting
learn to bear a burden
weightless as eternity.

TIME'S FOOL

Ocean's always more than we can make of it,
a better metaphor than any for two-handed time.

Swashbuckle, yes, and silver spears shaking,
that's how it was at the top of the tide,

but each wave breaking grew reluctant
to sort shingle, dissolve casts, even to adjust

that scribble of froth and stringy weed,
seacoal, mermaids' purses, bottles, brattlings.

Tide on the drag (after the equipoise)
lays bare our whole expanse of days

– momentary migrants reflected in water,
skimming over the foreshore, its shallows

and snags, hidden clear-eyed pools –
and then it summons from the deep

raven Thought, cormorant Memory.
Before tide's down and out, sandflats and slakes

become teeming wordbeds, salty and lucent,
where it's time always to address time.

SACRAMENTAL

We could commit the whole day
to this heavenly squelch
beyond the muddy paths and sour pans
cracking into soft, salt-bleached
mosaics. We'd try to match
what Latin names we remember
to the bristle-and-cocoon footing
this ocean of musty sea-lavender:

(Shadow-sweep: a marsh harrier.)
Saltmarsh grass and sea blite,
samphire twigs, almost luminous;
stands of sea purslane and red fescue.
(Taste of silt and sharp iodine.)
Here's a bone-house of sally crabs,
and a wicked witch's purse,
spikes we've never seen before...

What happens in this all but silent space,
preceding thought, inviting it,
is never simple, always changing.
An oystercatcher's *kleeep*. Sucks. Sighs.
Each sound or movement of what's hidden
signifies. Look! This shining shrimp
– leaping opal! The word on the tip
of your tongue may be sacramental.

FRENCH LEAVE

Sometimes the neap is surreptitious,
so soft so steady there's neither swill
nor suck as she slides into the muddy
staithe and lifts skiffs on their anchors,
shifting, out-eager, dreaming of searoom.

Just a jasmine smudge and a dozen
stars, a few marsh birds still conferring.
Three boys on the jetty, shoulder to shoulder.
Low voices, each daring the others.

They can hear the punch, the pound,
distant, arhythmical, and the shingle
cracking. Tide's almost on the ebb
again, they can see the red eyes
winking. The coast is quite clear.

MOCK MEDIEVAL: BRANCASTER BEACH

This lesser barbican, kin to some vast stronghold,
already looked ancient when it was young.
One face of the bastion collapsed, in fact,
while the builders were still on site,
but it boasted a redoubtable keep,
most ornately decorated, a deep moat
and, improbably, a minaret.
On its gritty haunches it sat,
scarcely less staunch than Bamburgh
or some brick-and-mortar shore fort,
facing foursquare across the German Ocean.

Clammy the dungeon and mightily constricted.
Carting and thumping and caressing,
three maidens down there with a little lad
(all four scantily clad) laboured to reinforce
the oozing walls. Full of dread and desire,
they exhorted one another with shrieks
and squeals, aware that even a short delay
was the best they could hope for.
Such innocent and willing victims
of the shining moon, the deadly god,
driven to their own destruction.

NORFOLK

Pick a likely lane
not one that blows open all the way to sea
but the kind with a green ridge,
heading inland, promising to twist
and quite possibly bring you back
within a mile or so
of where you began.
Maybe you'll pass beneath the shadow
of the gallows tree – the last in the county –
or the manor house (Elizabethan)
that escaped Pevsner
whose owners still retain a butler,
then around those tipsy ruins
of The Wind on the Moon,
these and perhaps a magic orchard
of Norfolk Peaches and then,
little smaller than an Olympic pool,
a slurry lagoon.

THE TIDE

On her way out, as she almost always is
this high up the muddy creek, so far
from the wailing and gleeful ocean.

What's revealed would be mostly
better hidden – stinking dregs, a midden
such as miserable Grimes wallowed in –

all but one furious inspector,
white of white, infinitely patient,
then thrusting and stabbing.

*

First light, celadon in the south-east.
No sooner is the spirit-tide
down and out than on the make again

with the north wind riding her, rock
and knock, slap against the bitten
stanchions abutting the Hard.

Now she's summoning the stars and
they're bursting into her. Light of light.
Still secretive, salty, all-possessing

YOUR SEA-VOICE

in memoriam Richard Murphy 1927-2018

When I heard you'd died, I'd no idea
we would meet for a second time.
I'd called in fifty years ago
at Derek's bidding (or Michael's?)
en route for Inishmore. All morning
we devoted to monks, penance, islands
and then you jolted me over to Omey
and Saint Fechin's pink granite ruins.
That's where you told me, and wept
as you told me, about the double sorrow.
We sheltered in a sandy hollow
under the first stars, weighed by all
that's fated and inescapable.

You're younger now, you say.
All day I've been scouring this trove
of your early verse for tell-tale signs
– dark histories, nightmares begun.
night drinking dark bog-pools
and *drowning is quick* and *wild graveyards;*
the soaked faces of the burnt out men
and their charred Armada wreck
plunges its rusty flukes into my heart,
but there's no more than I expected.

The wind's at worst boisterous,
showers spark, then they're gone,
and what I hear so very clearly
is your persuasive sea-voice,
what I watch is your hand steady
as the boom lifts, and the boat
drops, and above my knees the surge departs, departs...
Yes, much younger, you say, and sailing
to Tir-na-n-Og before nightfall.

THE NORTHERN GODS

Can you hear, dear Daisy,
that rousing horn and the deer-hide drum,
those distant bells on the high pastures?
Can you see that fiddler without a fiddle,
hoicking up his baggy trousers,
singing syllables and beginning to dance?
Listen! That yoik, summoning, capturing
a loved one or a favourite animal, a secret
glade cradled between rock shoulders.

I suspect you think there's very little to be said
for the northern gods, but let me translate them
into their makers, or even into your own
acquaintance. Think of some friend like Bragi
with a gift for poetry; or someone like Frigg
who – excuse my Latin – is a *mater familias;*
some old salt accustomed to iron rations.
A corn-silk blonde? A heavy drinker?
A woman driven by her instincts and passions?

Home from the halls and highlights of Asgard,
I think you'd be smitten by the gods' readiness
to take risks and laugh at themselves,
and admire their unflinching curiosity.
Their rampant sexuality might not be to your liking
but you'd be exhilarated by their energy and wit.
Maybe their childlikeness would disarm you
and you'd mourn at how, gods as they were,
they were fatalists, trapped in time.

Not only this. Look for the lines between lines.
Black scarves swirling, sweeping over tundra,
black grit smoking and scorching boot soles,
black bears, polar bears, packs of wolves,
mountain hares zigzagging across the glaciers
while the midnight sun bounces along the horizon
but then disappears for weeks on end.
Each fire flickers in its own hearth.
Nothing is ever easy on Middle Earth.

Have you ever dreamed you were sitting in the bole
of Yggdrasill, squinting up at the skull
of the white sky, then down into the icy swirl?
Have you heard the vitriol of the dragon,
the corpse-devourer, and seen how the squirrel
whisks it up to the eagle on the topmost branch?
And if, chaste and questing, you too were able
to sip water from the spring, would you
be prepared to make some great sacrifice?

'But the Vikings,' you say, wrinkling your nose,
'weren't they clannish and boastful and suspicious?'
Yes, but these are the defects of virtues.
Remember *Havamal*. 'Never be the first
to strain and break the bonds of friendship...
Never abuse a guest, and be generous
to anyone in need... If you know of some evil,
ensure everyone knows about it... A better man
often comes off worse when swords start talking.'

'What about their violence, then? Their brutality?'
(You persist so prettily). 'What about the blood eagle?'
By all means compare the habits of men and women
a millennium ago with contemporary values
but be very cautious... Can you imagine
what the Vikings would have said about us?
Come now, Daisy. Listen to the words
of a white-haired singer. Allow Idun
to tempt you with her apples, forever young.

The breath of her. Aliénor is always here
or hereabouts, trailing her wailing
retinue of troubadours.
                    In the love-garden
there's just one orchid, thin as a pencil-lead
(her tress spiralled overnight) with tiny blossoms,
almond-scented,
                    also a single bloom
on the Magnolia Grandiflora – the grandest
in Europe! – luscious and waxen. Before the bride
and her groom departed, there were five,
and one in bud.
                    These, and the bewitching
butterfly-maiden with eyes deep for drowning,
gliding like an acolyte several inches
above the ground.
                    The old leaf showed
his colours only at the last moment
– mottled stone and oaken, dark eye spots.
Then he trembled and faded through a gap
in the crumbling wall.
                    Knowing so very little
about Saint Félicien (without confusing him
with cheese or wild beasts) and not even having
seen his little finger, how can we be so sure
we belong to him, and he to us?
                    Imagine,
of course. Connect. But falsify nothing.
The suck-and-growl of the pool.
Black holes. Blossoms silently exploding.
The cloister censed by roses.
                    The rondel
of the seasons seems to spin faster, but I see
now there's nothing isolate, nothing.
All's well beyond words, presently singing.

Just down the lane those angels with wing-lifts
– two teams of eleven – are strutting their stuff
and in the aisles and on the benches
the coloured substitutes are blowing trumpets,
swinging censers like hammer-throwers,
and waiting their opportunity to muscle in.

These are their recumbent elder sisters
and taciturn brothers, gone grey at the temples.
Growing up in this place, they grew into it
and at dusk, peering down from the roof,
watching you for a little longer than you
watch them, they're reluctant to be picked out.

Though I scarcely knew you, I came to think
of you as one of these wise brethren,
self-effacing, fair in deed and Faire in name.
You kept your own church afloat through storms
and seasons and, almost eighty years ago,
built your own boat, the first here to do so.

First to fathom deep water, first to put
things right with a wink, always first
with the family pot of glue… And now
you've gone, though scarcely far, people keep
telling me of all the ways you're here
like a circle widening on bright water.

Isn't this exactly what we need and long for?
Servers not self-servers, not celebrities
but not Trappists either: more women
and men prepared to show not tell
– strands of shining gossamer, obstinate
and enduring, as all true angels are.

RICHARD LONG AT HOUGHTON

1. The Magician

Balls of gnats are spinning in the slanting
sunlight, a jet is white-painting
parallel lines, and fourteen people
are standing in a silent circle

watching an old man with a grimy handkerchief
knotted over his head lay slate
after slate in a spiral. He tamps them,
stamps on them (the ground here is uneven),

and it is growing. If they hold their ground
it could whirlpool around them, and they
would become what it is, sweet water
and force. Nothing is impossible.

Clack and clatter! They're listening,
half-dazzled by the shine and sheen,
fourteen apprentices to this wild dream
– this spellbinding, everyday magic.

2. WHITE WATERFALL

As when, early, with dew thick on the grass,
a web of gossamer criss-crosses the lawn,
        delicate as lace :

each waterfall here, created but never touched
(mud, energy and space), flows not only to the next
        but home to us.

Begin here perhaps. Is this monster the child
of our own terrors, and our intolerance?
        Is this quiver a ghost?

And is this the head of a dreaming, distant hill
crowned with trees, each branch still articulate
        – oak and beech and ash?

Are these our own arteries, our tendrils
and nerves and cells and ventricles?
        Such finesse!

Each waterfall seethes with sparks and star-splatter,
(accident and gravity). This is how we simplify
        and coalesce.

And laying my words here on these lines,
let me make my marks but lightly,
        and leave with grace.

3. X Marks the Spot

Crux: unignorable.

Armies of slates, ragged and jagged, not dove.
Pewter. Steel.

Glittering *chevaux de frise*: You could no more
cross it without laceration than cross a field
bristling with barbed wire.

Not Calvary. Not Tau, and not Swastika.
 X marks the spot.

Lord of the Four Winds. His lair.

Resting-place for skulls of kings and heroes.

Station. Boundary marker. Fiery not weeping.

Is this nightmare or clean sweep? A dawn
beginning?

Cross your fingers. Everything. Cross your heart.

4. Full Moon Circle

Half this globe is in the dark,
one quarter always advancing
or at war with another.

At my feet the wavelets lap,
they clip and slap each other, and
in the offing they half-open their jaws.

Or is this circle our own field-map
hymned by the sun, the seas of the moon,
each blade and slate ordaining:

'It's late, but still not too late.
Our poor planet. Care for her.
Care for her and she'll care for you.'

JAMES TURRELL'S *SKYSCAPE*

When the oaks stood aside
we stepped into a glade
where white deer glide
inside their dreams. Beyond
lay the giantesses, shining
and voluptuous, open to caresses.

We came to a wooden tower
and a skyhigh chamber
with benches along the walls,
recliners almost. A leaf drifted in.
Grey wisps unravelling.
Bottomless ocean, upside down.

Houghton Hall

1. Gravity for Beginners

Set aside theories and fearsome equations,
likewise galaxies, even saltwater tides.

Gravity is simply mutual attraction.

Words slipping into the mind's casket,
quick rain falling to attending earth.

2. Levity for Latecomers

Nothing to do with Leviathan, no
and nothing to do with frivolity.

Before we level with hydrogen consider Ralegh:

Hee gave to every nature his proper forme;
the forme of levitie to that which ascended.

WINTER AS IT USED TO BE

Such desire for your hands shining
in the flame's shadow:
their scent of oak and roses,
and death. Winter as it used to be.

Birds flew in searching for seed
and all at once became snowflakes;
as words do.

A burst of sunlight, an angel's aureole,
and then mist; and the trees,
and our singing selves, made of morning air.

LIKE THIS

Your dear hands, more especially
your bony wrists, describing how,
at the very last moment
before landing, pink-footed geese
correct their direction, like this,
and divers have to skelter
across water to take off – and how,
at sunrise, ten thousand knots
lifted from the saltmarsh
at Snettisham, and swirled their scarfs,
like this, and then the climbing sun
gilded and blackened them,
and held them to her breast.

SISTERING: DUBAI CREEK

Each old woman bears her shining moon
– one copper, one amber, one nacreous –
and places it gently on the damask.
Their table is well-laid; nothing is wanting.

crescents and quarters at their feet

This is their first night watch. Heads bowed,
the young women sit so still, so close
in their wheel of fears and secrets,
and each clasps her unborn baby.

the breathing water drags and makes

Within their ring of blinking lights,
shoulder to shoulder, thigh to thigh,
the girls plump down on the warm sand.
They cry for the moon, they laugh, and sing.

crescents and quarters at their feet,
the breathing water drags and makes

Sea suckled me, waves sounded over me,
rollers covered me as I rested on my bed…

'In this little sieve – this screen – you're looking
at four hundred thousand seeds. Yes, ma'am!
A quarter inch deep, at the very most.'

I've no feet, and often I open my mouth
to the flood…

'No, ma'am. Have a look through this microscope:
dozens of moons, wobbling,
all those legs, skedaddling.'

… sooner or later some man
will scoff me who gives not a toss for my shell…

'Now look at this chuckle here in my hands.
These little guys have each attached themselves
to a tiny piece of shell-grit.'

With the point of a knife he'll rip my skin
away from my side…

'Next month we bed them in the lagoon.
Then we harden them off in the Sound.
Call it the orchestration of a natural process.'

and at once eat me uncooked as I am…

'No, ma'am. Any time!
The outcome is just the same.'

Lopez Island

AS IT IS

Fitful sunlight. Dry rain, each spark
before it alights evaporating.

Scent of what? Dust, bitterbrush,
wild roses pink-pale,
maybe cow parsnip (sic),
needles of fir and Ponderosa:
a composite ancient and sacrosanct,
this ground's memory.

Delete the fanciful.
Tell each component simply as it is.
Grace precedes significance.

Thus: at the top of the dark gully,
one white Alpine butterfly
with a purple gland, three petals
pointed, three frayed...
This scorching paintbrush
rough to my fingertips...

Mare's tails curl high and deep
over Hozemeen and Methow Valley,
the many-tongued river
plunges down from the glacier.

Another dazzle.
A goldfinch starts to dance,
and my own ghost-shadow
stages a comeback.

The far bank is frozen and corrugated,
it drops to water stagnant, winter-curdled,
jammed with sodden leaves, delicate bones
and Oasis cans; the near bank is springloaded
with sharp-eared aconites and snowdrops.
There's shrill whistling in the brakes
and screaming in the air, white wings tacking,
making heavy weather of it.

Stumbling along the bilious hedgerows
half-strangled with glistening ivy,
one fellow is wearing a feathered hat
and one shouldering his accordion…
Most have seen it before, and they all
know the way of it, this war
across the common stream.
Three o'clock. The third Sunday in February.

Advancing along either bank, everyone
comes face to face below the crumbling
horsebridge where Bucks and Oxon meet
– the place where as children they played
poohsticks and swore blood secrets –
as many as either village can muster,
but well down on last year's numbers.
The great grey trunks soar over them.

Scuffing beech mast, staring into sky-pools
above and below them, each side unties
the rope hitched to a branch. There's room
for everyone, laughing and jostling.
Nothing stretches as long as time
before beginning, but at last the front men
fall silent. They dig in their heels
as if the seasons of their lives depend on it.

At first the two teams give not an inch.
They lurch, they grunt, and their coaches
synchronise each haul, each stay.
Perched on the steep shoulders
of the bridge their supporters howl.
But now, on the far bank, the first man
slithers down the mud-slide on his butt
and his whole line has to give ground.

What happens? How do they recover,
and then regain much more than they lost?
Muscle, sheer bloody-mindedness.
Their new coach? A new dispensation?
On the near bank, the leader slips
through snowdrops, the second staggers
over him, and half the team are dragged,
shouting and swearing, into the stream.

Commotion. Confusion. But after
the flurry, all the stabilising rituals
hold – the contestants climb up and crowd
on to the bridge, pink and sweating;
and, as usual, the accordion's time has come.
Wind-shear. Roaring beeches. Needles of rain.
They shout and laugh, and raise glasses
of damson wine to the absent sun.

Suspicion, though, feeds on itself,
and many folks reckon it's all a fix.
Why, the outcome's been the same
for as long as anyone can remember.
Some people are blaming the fearsome winter,
some climate change, most just don't know.
There's to be a joint parish meeting but, even so,
how can things ever be natural again?

HOW YOU SEE, I SEE

I wait in my writing-room,
Its window streaked by rain.
Lavender wands splay in the gloom.
Moths press against the pane.

One blink! Here you are again,
Making light of my life,
Converting study into den,
Slicing with my paperknife

And picking out pink paperclips,
Smiling up, then sliding down,
Parting your pretty lips,
Dancing with Phil Cunningham.

Half-child, half-sprite,
flitting and wild and grave.
I see you see yourself, and write
How you see, I see, and we wave.

MY MOTHER'S INKPOT

When I severed the top joint of my left thumb
I opened the floodgates. My children's children
shrieked, and for much of that afternoon I built
churches with steeples, and conjured shining coins
out of air, and retaught my rheumatic fingers
to fashion snapping shadow-monsters.
Mah-zheek! they cried. *Mah-zheek! More!*

When my father performed much the same sleights,
my mother often sat at her marquetry desk
and dashed off letter after letter, all wit
and fervour. She regarded a wide margin
or an untouched inch in the way
a gardener might view an unsown drill
or border – an opportunity wasted.

Over and again she drained the deep well dry
but never once was I magicked by that,
not until the morning after she'd invited me
to refill it – silver, quietly gleaming.
I saw how the heavy lid had lifted.
This posy of primulas, lemon and orange,
were springing and spilling out of it.

HERE, ON THE HEADLAND

Here, on the headland
lifted last week
and still unploughed,
I scooped up dusty seedlings
that had slipped through the grader
– sufficient for a meal or two –
and stuffed my pockets.

Then in the topmost corner
where tattered hedgerows meet
I found little heaps
almost the size of molehills
raised but dropped
when the turning harvester
sloughed them off.

Incomparable, I thought,
for any observer:
here in the wings, half-curtained,
yet still in light of light
with a sightline right down
to the foreshore and the anchorage
– pale eucharists at my feet.

EN ROUTE

Isn't there always some unscheduled halt
with its attendant wonders? Now and then
the marvellous or the monstrous
but more often the humdrum
– a reclamation yard, or the smell
of an autumn bonfire; this siding, say,
choked with dusty purple nettles,
an ochre butterfly flickering over them.

Even the weathered inspector
is half-surprised, half-smiling
at your single, steadfast gaze.
Whatever is. Maybe early, very likely
late, you know this is the one true line
and now you're well en route.

VERGANGENHEITSBEWÄLTIGUNG

Well, if you say so!
I know my words

have often been flighty
so I've pinioned these

with this octosyllable

beneath a dove-grey
cobble stone, a memorial

I lifted in 1968
from a kerb in Prague.

Soon after Albano hoicked his sheep into the bath of his three-bedroom house in Cherry Hinton and cut its throat, we parted company.

My verse, *Nomads*. That's how we met. I recall not a single line, but he was taken with the rough-and-toughness and terseness of it.

And that's how he saw himself. Stocky. Battling. Stamping out his staging-posts.

A Resistance leader.

Champion of causes. Hitch-hiking. Karagiosis. Mandatory Mandarin in all secondary schools.

Half-bald, head like a cannon-ball.

His poem for his mother made me squirm. My eyeballs burned. Our shared room was too small.

Architect of churches too roseate for the Home Counties: of his deceased Italian father, he spoke very little.

So very generous. Above all, the way he threshed my poems and blitzed my translations.

So scornful. On the back of an envelope he mapped my progression: *Faber Poetry Editor. Poet Laureate. Knighthood.* (Well, no, none of those!) 'Is that really all you want?'

The last letter I had from him was after his Pinochet protest and release from the football stadium in Santiago.

Did we not have a single friend in common?

His birthday gift: a precious edition of *Cuchulain of Muirthemne*, inscribed 'For Kevin, to stop him selling this'.

Each gave and took what he needed. So what was I to him? Younger brother, acolyte, itching post. Still so unquestioning and so hidebound, not quite unredeemable.

Moth memories? No. Grappling-hooks.

When his wife wrote years later, I was unable to answer, unable to throw her words away.

Never a green boy – a student, say,
of coppicing and bud-burst, never a disciple
of the nomad bodgers, propped half the day
against a bavin – but the way he fingertipped
to the fork in his climbing-tree, high above
all the initials and graffiti, and reached
upwards as beeches do...
                  Aged nine,
he staged a protest beneath the doomed
trees at Ladymede, and cried when he heard
the terrible grinding. Their toppling haunted
him, and for years he dreamed that beech trees
were growing into him.
               How each leaf
looks like its selfsame tree, and the way
its roots brace; kinship, intelligence,
spelter and the principles of turning,
– yes, of course he was eager to find out
all these things, but later.
               Mid-April.
It's very mild, almost still, one by one at last
the leaves are falling. Each twists, though,
or spurts forward, or slides in mid-tango,
loops, maybe rises again. As he lunges
after them, the old man laughs, stumbles
and begins to name them.
                Copper and Rust,
Shy, Sideways, Surge, Lonesome, Only,
Wounded, Wonder, Wanderer, Tawny Gold,
Trickster, Memory.

THE NEW FAMILIAR

It's always the same, and never.
Under our feet the ground starts
to heave, the skyline becomes toothy,
and soon there'll be that first sight
of snow, is it, all of fifty miles off,
unless it's only limestone.

Our host conducts us up wide steps
scalloped by centuries of hooves
and halfway along the cloister corridor,
then swings open *Les Coquelicots*.
Trumpet sunlight. Welcoming shadows.
Leaving leisurely, he says, there's to be
a trip tomorrow morning to hunt
for wild orchids, 'and a great surprise
this year'. Would we care to come?

We've crossed half this continent again
and arrive at this: what we crave
is no longer the unbelievable,
the idyllic or hitherto inaccessible
– not the old imperatives beyond
the horizon, but the new familiar.

THROUGH A GLASS, DARKLY

Tumbleweed somersaults, it bundles right
along the dreadful rim. But in a stone hide
we stumbled on an old brass reflectoscope
– black onyx, darkened glass – and saved
ourselves from the worst of our atrocities.

Unless you're a demon or some temptress
why on Earth would you look down not up?
Peering through fingers into appalling depths
(five thousand million years of gneiss and schist)
desolate, flooded, cancerous, burning.

Far better to look up. Raise your eyes
to cloud-castles, light on the mountains,
silver ghost-paths of dream and intention.
Unlimited by flesh or bone, the gods
have never lived in ditches or craters.

Yet even so, with our tarred soles and muddy
hands, there'll be no blinding revelation.
We can only watch for what we may
not see or, if we do, just glimpse
through soothing shades, and bear witness.

RECONCILIATION

I'm no flat earthist, but don't dispute
the world's four corners have been held up
by dwarfs, which has nothing whatsoever
to do with the Four Corners monument,
which has nothing to do with the
petrified gods of the Navajo and Vikings.

How entrancing the mind is,
crossing so hungrily between planes,
wrestling with the complex and knowing
when to suspend disbelief, and how
to reconcile opposites, accepting
that answers always beg questions.

And yet to sit for an hour or so
beside this turbulent salt creek
and watch a cloud of dark knots
flying as one, or hear the single yap
of rigging responding to what I cannot
even see: this is homecoming.

It's true, nothing is irreconcilable
but, far from unhopeful, the old mind
begins to tire, no longer as restless
as this tide on the make, always
insistent (despite the dams
and groynes) on its links and passages.

In the blue hour, a single prayer suffices.

SHOULDER ON

Even if there's any reason why this
has happened, there's no need to reason why.
Better to regard it as a kind of blessing
like a next-to-neap tide stealthily
replenishing the drained, muddy creek,
or the last red-gold on a far field.

Isn't it an invitation to engage
while you can, aware each word
and silence entail responsibilities?
Accept interruptions. Shoulder on.
Try again to say something worth saying
without knowing yet quite what it is.

SILENT ORDER

Words again. Words.
How am I to put them
in service to silence?

The stretch-fields here
are so rich with promises,
memories, never endings.

Silver-green with flint arrowheads,
golden with proud
and finicky bones,

Or look at the rage,
the flags and rags of oaks
only last year stricken,

the daily drumroll of clouds
towering and threatening,
gentling into dusk showers.

Let me absorb all this
and begin again. Let me commit
to the slow work of unsaying.

True, what I've tried to say
– there's no gainsaying it,
but this unravelling, this denying

myself years of stitchwork,
and all I never questioned
I was born to do…

No longer to sing, to share,
obedient only
to this one calling.

LA PLAINE DE LA MADELEINE

Well above the hamlet on its tipsy ledge
there was a meadow. One path scrambled up to it.
It was passionate with wildflowers and unvisited,
innocent of whatever was happening below.
On hands and knees I crawled along the side
where you could drop off the edge of the world.

Long ago, waking hot and hectic
or shocked by some dream, I used to splash
my face with water biting as a mountain stream,
lie back and climb that rocky path again.
Turbanned lily, gentian, orange poppy,
soldanella… names I no longer remember.

Each breathing midnight now, unsure I'll return,
I realise I'm doing the same. I'll do the same.

IN A NORFOLK GARDEN

An Idyll for Peter Scupham and Margaret Steward

Little clusters of guests are sitting
beneath the tortured oaks, a few on tartan rugs,
most on the jaundiced grass,
and others are lined up on recliners
like survivors from some TB sanatorium
soaking in this late August sunlight.
Something's going on in front of them:
a pair of ancients, gesticulating.
Their backs are turned but I can hear
their words, even at this distance.
> *Jesu, Jesu, the mad days that I have spent!*
> *And to see how many of my old acquaintance*
> *are dead... We shall all follow, cousin...*
Got it! It's those two country justices.
> *Certain, 'tis certain; very sure, very sure.*

*

While I'm still listening to these two truth-tellers,
hollow-eyed and glum, playing at playmaking,
a wizened monk, maybe a Carthusian
or some Carmelite home from the Holy Land,
grabs my collar.
> *'Norfolk!'* he croaks,
'Norfolk! Satan on the road to Hell
ruined Norfolk as he fell.' His breath
smells of honey. I readjust my sprig
of sea-lavender, and politely refer him
to Sir John who's on his way
with his old flame, Billa,
and expected around teatime.

*

Over there, that's George Barker,
black drill-eyed, well oiled already
and the sun's not yet at the zenith.
He's hectoring the pinstripe murderer
who awarded me a bar to my DFC,
then finished me off at Biggin Hill,
presently strangling a very pretty
young whitebeam with his spider fingers.
Why are they pincering poor George Szirtes?
What's going on? Is this some nomen league,
celebrants of a tribune martyred
in Nicomedia, venerated only
in England, Portugal and Albania?

*

Surrounded by cats and herbs, mossy statues
and stagnant little pools fringed with white lace,
what grows in this sacred space
are words, well-watered, thinned
and pleached and flowering – year upon year
of readings and recitations grave and gay
by lights very bright and distinctly limited,
generations of poets, some with their families,
attending to their roots and calling.

*

You'd heard that several guests had died,
some long since, and that's the case,
but it's scarcely surprising to be surrounded
by like minds and 'affable presences'.
Almost everyone's present at this assembly
they wouldn't miss for anything.

Look! There's Skelton, our first laureate, rapping
with a young man who spent all morning
choosing which cravat to wear
(mauve, yes, mauve, I think so), and then how to tie it.
But who's that with bells on his ankles,
hopping and skipping between the weedy beds
and warbling in his annoying falsetto:

> *A Country Lasse browne as a berry…*
> something, something… *heart as merry,*
> *Cheekes well fed and sides well larded*
> *Every bone with fat flesh guarded…*

Got it again! It's Will Kemp,
darling of the groundlings
and dancer all the way from London to Norwich,
his eyes always sharp for the next chance,
a 'Marrian in his Morrice daunce'.

*

As for Old Hall, and its 'long marriage
of queen strut, king post, its mysteries
'exposed by sweat, patched together with lime,
stage-paint, a little imagination',
let it rest today on its laurels.
Our paths lead out from it,
all our words come home to it
and its 'gatekeepers and custodians'.
Everyone here knows that.

> *Love it. Choose it. Whatever the words mean*
> *Hauled from the moil, the tumult in the head*
> *And heart.*

*

Our host rises, gleaming and genial,
bent double almost. First he rehearses a few
regrets and no-shows, among them Frances Cornford,
Lilias Rider Haggard and dear Wystan,
then announces a couple of surprise arrivals:
two more Georges, on horseback,
both from silly Suffolk. Very strange.

> *When tides were neap, and, in the sultry day,*
> *Through the tall bounding mud-banks made their way,*
> *Which on each side rose swelling, and below*
> *The dark warm flood rose silently and slow...*

Ah, Crabbe! George Crabbe, my words, hard-won,
echo your own. My creeks and staithes of Brothercross,
their small gains shored against struggle and loss...

*

The quick and the dead,
home-grown and foreigner,
seventeen poets now stand and deliver.
Several of them are audible.
Sail, and Mole of Mandeville,
and Brownjohn, Griffiths, Underwood,
and last, as befits our senior poet:

> *Speaking as best I may, or as I might.*
> *If the day failed and all there was was night,*
> *I look for something which could still be light.*

Yes, that's Anthony Thwaite.
It's very nearly too late.

*

65

'Where's William Cowper?' I ask my host.
'My namesake on my mother's side.
'A sage beneath a spreading oak.'

He gives me a melancholy look. 'Is that so?
'I don't rightly know. Neither does he.'

*

This blistering heat. These tumblers of red wine.
Butterfly flicker…
Dear creatures, marinade those hours.
Where, pray, in this whole kingdom
is there any living ancient place,
any garden trained, still wild, a dream
of an assembly in the least like this?

Old Hall Poetry Picnic, South Burlingham

p. 9 Epigraph Rilke: 'Der Sänger Singt vor einem Fürsten-kind'.

p. 13 'Seahenge: A Journey': dedicated to Andrew Rafferty. Seahenge was a timber circle. It consisted of 55 split oak trunks and at its centre was a huge oak stump, upside down. It was constructed in 2049BCE and discovered, standing on the foreshore near Holme in Norfolk, in 1999. In poems 3-6, a young woman tells how she helped to build the circle and lay the body of her father within it.

p. 24 'Time's Fool': written in response to Shakespeare's Sonnet 60, 'Like as the waves make towards the pebbled shore.'

p. 25 'Sacramental': for Linda.

p. 30 'Your Sea-Voice': quotations from *Archipelago 12* (Summer, 2019) and *Sailing to an Island* (Faber, 1963).

p. 31 'The Northern Gods': for Daisy Jellicoe.

p. 34 'L'Abbaye-Château de Camon': the village of Camon is in Aude, within sight of the Pyrenees. The medieval fortified house and Abbey adjoin one another.
Aliénor: Eleanor of Acquitaine.
Félicien: patron saint of the Abbey.

p. 35 'In North and South Creake': in memoriam Richard Faire.

p. 41 'Levity for Latecomers': Sir Walter Ralegh *The History of the World* (1614).

p. 42 'Winter as it Used to Be': translated with Richard Barber's assistance from Salvatore Quasimodo.

p. 45 'These Little Guys': the lines in italics are translated from riddle 77 (oyster) in the 11th century Exeter Book.

p. 46 'As It Is': for Mary Siemon and Sern Watt. The poem is set in the North Cascades.

p. 47 'Tug-of-War': for many years there has been an annual summer tug-of-war across the River Thame between the villages of Ickford in Buckinghamshire and Tiddington in Oxfordshire.

p. 53 'Vergangenheitsbewältigung': a marvellous German compound, meaning 'coming to terms with the past'.

p. 63 'In a Norfolk Garden': italicised quotations by William Shakespeare; anonymous; Will Kemp; Peter Scupham; George Crabbe; Anthony Thwaite. For Peter Scupham and Margaret Steward.

ACKNOWLEDGEMENTS

'Time's Fool' formed part of *On Shakespeare's Sonnets: A Poets' Collection* edited by Hannah Crawforth and Elizabeth Scott-Baumann and was published by Bloomsbury in association with the Royal Society of Literature, Shakespeare 400 and King's College, London (2016).

The poems in the Richard Long sequence were commissioned by the Marquess of Cholmondeley and Houghton Hall as part of *BeLong*, an educational project coinciding with Earth Sky: Richard Long at Houghton, 2018.

'Sacramental' and 'Your Sea Voice' were first printed in *Agenda*; 'As it Is' in *Ambit*; 'French Leave' in *Archipelago*; 'These Little Guys' in *Gallery* edited by Tabitha Hayward (St. Edmund Hall, Oxford, 2017); 'Crossing', 'Tides' and 'Burden' were first printed in *Resurgence*; 'Norfolk' was first printed in *Rialto*; 'Beeches' in *Smoke*, 'La Plaine de Madeleine' and 'Reconcilation' and 'Winter as it Used to Be', in *Temenos Academy Review*; 'Shoulder On' in *The New European*, 'Silent Order' in *Theology* and 'The Northern Gods' in *The Vikings Reimagined* edited by Tom Birkett and Roderick Dale (de Gruyter, 2019).

Seahenge: A Journey was first published by Kailpot Press in 2019 with photographs by Andrew Rafferty.

KEVIN CROSSLEY-HOLLAND is a poet, translator from Anglo-Saxon, librettist, reteller of traditional tales including the Norse myths, and prize-winning historical novelist for children. He has collaborated with the artists Norman Ackroyd and Chris Riddell and with many composers including Nicola LeFanu and Bob Chilcott, and, most recently, with Cecilia McDowall on their acclaimed cantata *The Girl from Aleppo*. Kevin Crossley-Holland has been awarded honorary doctorates by Anglia Ruskin and the University of Worcester, and he is an Honorary Fellow of St. Edmund Hall, Oxford, a Patron (and Past President) of the School Library Association, the Society for Storytelling and the Story Museum, and a Fellow of the Royal Society of Literature. The Brotherton Library at Leeds University will be mounting an exhibition of his archive in summer 2021, the year in which he celebrates his eightieth birthday.